Susan A. Katz has been reading, writing, publishing, and loving poetry for over 50 years. She finds inspiration for her poems in the everyday business of living, of family joys and sorrows, and in the vast and wondrous landscape of the natural world. She conducted poetry workshops for poets in public service, and independently for over 30 years and has co-authored two textbooks on how to integrate the arts into school curriculums. Susan's poetry reveals her intense passion for the living quality of language, and she believes that "poetry is the need to write beyond the limits of choice; the freedom to see beyond the limits of light."

Susan A Katz
April / 2024

To Menke Katz:
Poet, philosopher, rabbi, teacher, a "real human being"
(1906–1991)
With my sincere thanks for allowing me
to share in the joy and beauty you found
in every minute of every day.

Susan A. Katz

DREAMING MISSOURI

AUSTIN MACAULEY PUBLISHERS™

LONDON • CAMBRIDGE • NEW YORK • SHARJAH

Ordering Information
Quantity sales: Special discounts are available on quantity purchases by corporations, associations, and others. For details, contact the publisher at the address below.

Publisher's Cataloging-in-Publication data
Katz, Susan A.
Dreaming Missouri

ISBN 9781649794444 (Paperback)
ISBN 9781649794451 (ePub e-book)

Library of Congress Control Number: 2021925853

www.austinmacauley.com/us

First Published 2022
Austin Macauley Publishers LLC
40 Wall Street, 33rd Floor, Suite 3302
New York, NY 10005
USA

mail-usa@austinmacauley.com
+1 (646) 5125767

Dan Masterson

A special, heartfelt thank you to poet, teacher, friend, Dan Masterson. In his classroom, in his living room, sipping wine with our families in the back yard, he taught me the true meaning of poetry, and gave me the greatest gift of all, belief in myself, as a poet.

Judith A. Thomas

Judith and I have been friends and creative colleagues ever since we met at Nyack Elementary School, in Nyack, New York, where I was conducting poetry workshops for Poets in Public Service, and Judith was the music teacher. Judith is a music specialist, so talented in so many ways it takes your breath away. Together we conducted workshops, with students and educators, for over thirty years and, co-authored two textbooks. She has been a true inspiration to me, and has given me insights into, and trust in, the creative process. I have been truly honored to have worked with her, and beside her, all these years.

Table of contents

Dreaming Missouri

Dreaming Missouri

Last night I dreamed
Missouri; it could
have been Wisconsin, I've never
been there either; it was
Missouri, because I think
I liked the way the word
unrolled across my tongue, slowly
like a distant siren fading
to the whisper
of the leaves,
once, I dreamed
adventure, stars, solar
eclipse, Atlantis
sinking, but I drowned
beneath a swell of tears
and screams until
I surfaced out
of sleep and let my eyes
believe the solid
feel of walls, the boundary
of ceilings; and so,
last night it was
Missouri, unnamed streets and faces

blank as tide washed sand.

Day moves precisely in
to night and nights
are races I must win; I fortify
myself with dreams as tame
as names of places
I have never been.

Memories of Maple

I

I want memories of maple
leaves that cup the dew
like small green hands,
skies blue as corn flowers
blossoming on Grandma's blouse; I want
to taste the morning
air thickened to the flavor of berries
hot in the sun, water
lurking cool in deep
shaded mountain pools.
I want memories of milk
still warm from the udder, no
glass container sweating
on the table; the thick
stroke of night sweeping across
open fields closing in a fist
around insistent dreams. I want
the memory of dirt black beneath
my nails, the feel
of worms warm in a wealth of soil.
I want to close my eyes and hear

bird songs, catch the scent of flowers
soft secrets in the heart of silent woods.

II

I am learning things too late,
names of things that sing
themselves; spirea, pyracantha,
fire-on-the-mountain; city girl
brought up in taffeta and patent leather
pumps, I hold memories of linen
and of lace; powdered faces, Grandma's
hair white and wistful, a prisoner
of pins and nylon net.
Summers at the country club I played
the game of meeting boys
with prospects, attended birthday parties,
where candles lit a landscape of pink icing,
marzipan roses too pretty
and too sweet to eat.
Winters found me wrapped in cashmere
and angora, perfumes
the color of deep amber, bottled
in graceful glass poised
on bathroom shelves, my room pleated
in pastel was framed by windows
burglar-proofed in steel.

III

Too late I spy my own reflection,
feel my texture sensible as denim,
inelegant, essential as the seasons.
Outside, autumn leaves
scream their death in raucous
tones of color torn
from reluctant limbs, memories
die unborn.

Almost Winter

It is almost winter; I wake
in the dark, begin
the chores that will take me
through the day, the room is chill,
the windowsill wet
with melting frost, a bird's
song breaks from the corner
of the yard, lonely, after summer's
rowdy chorus; behind
the pin oak and the scrub, sunlight
touches a still leafy willow.
I imagine the grip of winter
with its dead grey grass
showing through the snow,
icicles forming along the overhang
whorling in a continuous
melting and growing, grotesque
daggers that form shadow bars
along the window glass.
Years ago I raced
headlong into city snowstorms, wrapped
in layers of wilting wool,
waded into plowed piles beside

the buildings and imprisoned
cars until my fingers tingled
and my toes grew numb; steamed
inside the kitchen, the smell of wet wool
and cocoa suffocating as the radiator
puffed and groaned.
Now it's vague, like looking
at a painting of a place
you've never been, as though
we live quietly
connected lives, one following
the other; today, inside
my winter-insulated walls,
I hoard the remnants of those little
lives that came and went
and am content
to just stay warm.

Mid-Life

The world was ending in a splash
of liquid flame and we
were escaping; I don't know how,
there are ways that dreams
provide, but Mother called me
back and sent me crying
for her large bath towel
and pink satin pillowcase.

What would the doctors arched
over polished desks, think
of that? I can hear them
grimly scribbling back,
to childhood and the womb, Mother's
disintegrating in her tomb,
her dreams are dust.

These years we stand
at graves burying people and things.
Mother, in the spring. Now, she is vague
as vapor rising off the lake, a thin
veil of something I once knew
and cherished casually.

The children leave
their laundry on the floor, notes
on the counter, I jot lines of poetry
on the back of bank deposits
and grocery tapes and dream at night,
and wake with the uneasy feeling
that I had the chance, but never
got it right.

It's Ten P.M.

...and I don't know
where my children are; they
have hurtled the fences, wandered
out through the open
gate owning
themselves; now
I feel around
in empty pockets, rummage
in cluttered drawers, count
pennies I've collected, the sum
is staggeringly small.

Why is it we believe
the lies we tell
when comforting ourselves
to sleep: *time
and change extract
a reasonable cost.*

Beside the window watching
shadows rearrange
the empty street, it's ten p.m.
and I, not they, am lost.

Without Virtue

> "…mere distaste for horror is not
> some kind of virtue."
> – Judson Jerome
> *"ABHORRENT ACTS"*

I eat no meat, no red
meat packed in plastic
with a sanitary
pad to staunch the blood
still oozing long
after the butcher's knife
has changed the shape
of flank and thigh of hip
and belly into a line
that better fits
the pan; *"man, after all,*
must eat and what's alive
must, anyway, eventually die."
No more than seven, Grandma
Lizzie took me to the kosher
chicken farm, we eyed the
boisterous antics of the flock,
looking for (I swear I never

had the slightest inkling)
what; but soon, her less
than five-foot frame straightened
and her pointed finger aimed
and death squawked
and flapped
and bled and I
went dinner-less to bed.
Today, I am afraid
of bombs and terrorists
of rape and crack and acid rain
and cannot bear to hear
the newscast voices claim
the gore as glory; so, I live
mute within my poems and cause
no pain, and I believe
that virtue is not born
of abstinence or even
affirmation of a righteous
cause, but late
at night when light leaves
only memory of itself behind and dreams
are blind insinuations of the life
you lead, my dreams are whole,
unbutchered; they do not bleed.

The Other Side of Sky

I counted stars embedded
in the rich black soil
of sky. Their light was cold
and hard and distant as the seeds
that lay unseen beneath a frozen
winter white.
I wondered if
we lay beneath a landscape
vast beyond our dreams, looking
up into the roots of stars that
flower into light, if all that comes
within our mind and grasp is but a spot
of loam on some eternal plain.
For all our pomp and vain
delight in who and what
we are the night absorbs
our image easily
swallowing our substance and our shadows
leaving us anonymous, alone,
as though
we had not yet become what
we could be
if not in life, perhaps

in death we rise to blossom
on the other side of sky.

In the Place of Nothing

     – at 30,000 feet
Above the clouds, beneath
the vast expanse
of universe, we spread
ourselves across a vacancy
of sky,
not blue, but colorless
and empty
and elusive as the flames
that finger wood
to ash, leaving
nothing in the place
of something; nothing
stretched out and up
or down, beyond
this hole that is
the whole
of all eternity.
We invade the silence,
a silver scream that follows
lines connecting us
from where we've been
to where we need to go; as though

we know the comfort
to be found
in destinations.
Above the clouds, beneath
the vast expanse
of universe, we climb
the rungs of air and hover
for a moment in the endless
idling of time; something
in the place of nothing.

Dreaming Names and Dates and Places

Names and Dates and Places

– for my father

The voice that calls
from between fingers
of rain; leaps
along leaves, slips
through the netting
of screens, is it yours?
Does the blood bond blossom
anew in the thick
wet womb of summer?

Dreams were dry wood
collected for a fall
flame and pride fell
light as a feather; do I
dare believe your voice
putting the old words back
together again?
Did I tell you
how I hid
in the dark
listening? I disbelieved

in eyes that watched
you die, in fingers
that felt flesh
grow cold, in love
that proved no stronger
than a sigh.
Did I send you
something of myself; an offering
of tears and terror that wrung
memory dry; leaving
the years scattered
like seeds on unwelcoming
ground; albums
faithfully recorded names
and dates and places; no one
was ever really lost, nothing
ever left behind and I
settled myself in the shade
of familiar shadows.

Lately, time grows thin
and like the hawk
we move in circles
learning comfort
by coming back
to where we've been.
Out of August's dark rain
your voice grows
takes flight and spreads
wings over my name.

An Offering

– for my mother

I promised her poems
pages of poems ripe
as melons in July, fattening
in the long summer nights while
she slept behind burglar-safe bars
I lay with my back
to the window, apart, we broke
that way, falling away from each other.
She wondered if it would be
worth her while to die
for a poem, Momma, they have all
been for you.
You planted the rows more years ago
than even I remember,
hacked at the soil with a dull hoe,
never knew each word
each line, each bent and brittle
rhyme was a green-gold offering
to you, who had no time, no time.

Why She Died

– again for mother
Because she could no longer see
the sun; past care
or caring, locked in the cell
of her insanity she cursed
the doctors and cried
into the tapioca; too tough
she muttered and remembered
something that mattered.
Because in Long Beach ants
invaded the back porch she boiled
water, steam rising to curl
her hair and dumped it on them.
They died in hordes, black
bubbles rising to the surface
of that temporary
lake, already draining
through the boards.
Because there was no room left
in the family plot, we had to dig
the rhododendron out; by adding
her death to the rest, we tried
to make it matter less.

Father

Melodies were eased
out of the strings
of the mandolin by those
incredible fingers, we sang
to outdistance the tune
he knew them all
by heart.
They were promises
we meant to keep, who knew
new music would replace
the old, even
the children have forgotten
the songs that lulled them
to sleep.

Mother

(The Cheyenne Indians
called frost "the bones
of the rain")

Somber seasons, ghostly
grey and flat as faces
in sleep, keep
quiet promises; birds
come back to feed, juncos
and finches, pigeons and doves.
What little we knew
of you was all there was, not
the fullness of harvest, but
the restless turning of seeds
toward sun; like that,
expectant, we waited.
Through flamboyant springs,
red-breasted robins offering
song and wing-shaped leaves adorning
oak and willow; summers,
garish and ebullient, too colorful
to comprehend, through fall's

forgiveness, taking
back without remonstrance
or regret and winters,
stately as the white blaze
of candles at a coffin.
We learned you too late,
proud and permanent
as pain - spread out
between the seasons
like the broken bones
of rain.

The Wounded Years

– for Selma

The dust has settled like a hymn
over the memory of your eyes; dark and deep
as sorrow, blind
to all the passions that I couldn't name
that came over me in waves
of words I couldn't speak; we spoke
like swords, each interchange
a clash of separate wills that spilled
a bit of blood, a puddling of tears.
Who pays the price for all the wounded
years? What happens to the warriors when all
the wars are lost or won? What is the cost
to heroes whose names are but a lapse
of memory to the tongue? Who cares
for causes when the banners lay forgotten
lessons in the trampled mud?
What good are lessons now when time
has emptied you to silence, filled me
with a thousand small regrets.
I could have held your face
between my palms and stroked

your eyelids as they closed against
the light. I could have whispered
how the scars would heal beneath the sterile
layers of the night; I could have asked, humbly,
like a child
at prayer, forgiveness; and in return
offered never to unlearn you, to sing
you like a marching cadence through the hollow
victory of the years.

Aunt Esther at 100

She will turn to the wall
and sweat with the heat
of memory tucked
firmly under her chin,
it is at night
when darkness thickens
into paste, sheets sticking
to belly and thigh that things
come clear; too clear, like a lake
glassy and smooth, exposing
its grimy bottom.
Too much time
at night, hours long
and billowing deposit
broken promises and faces
on her pillow, hands rising
to offer consolation are bony
as bedposts.
She wakes often
to the sound of her own
voice, a pinched wail
that begins and ends
with silence. Sometimes she counts

backwards from a hundred or
rhymes words to keep
from thinking, but the night
outstays her and she sinks
defeated back
into August sheets.
It is not so much that memories
are sorrow, but the emptiness
that holds them
firmly in place is the space
she lives in and when
the floor creaks or timbers
settle in the humid air,
she cocks her head and calls
"is that you, are you there;" straining
with failing sight to see
beyond the black
casket of her bed.

Something of Stone

Her death is an itch
at the end of my fingertips...
    and still
    she does not die.
She shrivels like a plucked
peach, her eyes
flatten to yellow like tepid
tea or wilting dandelions.
Graves have announced themselves
in a plot crowded with the dead,
husbands, two of them, brothers,
sisters, whole generations
have passed her by,
flesh-eater, death-beater, old
woman carving out her days
with an ax-sharp tongue,
counting and recounting
her store of lace-edged nighties
and satin underdrawers, doling
out the bread a slice
at a time, incensed to find
the milk all gone; something
there is in her, something

of stone; fierce little mouse gnawing
at us, thriving
on the game, I soothe
my fingertips along the marble
tabletop and trace the outline
of her name.

Framed in Memory

Age whitened dull
as paste
around the corners
of your mouth
stuck fast
to sorrow, time
held you curling
toward death
like the browned
edges of photographs.
You had been
sitting for years, hands
lumped in your lap, eyes
tracing smiles frozen
on faces you had
framed in memory.

Aunt Liz and Uncle Joe

Her lap was big enough
for two and he knew how to hook
a worm so it stayed put; she believed
in things that she could see,
he liked
      to bend things
to his will, turn back the woods
that threatened to invade the lawn,
plug up a gopher hole or hack
at weeds before the sun was high,
we never
      heard her comment on how green
the grass, how tall the flowers grew,
and once, in play, we covered
up her eyes and asked him
what their color was, he said,
he didn't think he knew; after
a scrapbook
      full of years she died
before summer had fulfilled
itself, blossoms still undecided
on the vine; late September, watching
the grass shrivel and the trees

shake themselves bare,
he kicks
      the leaves and talks
to no one in particular about how capable
her fingers were and how
he liked the way she combed her hair.

Out of September

– for my sister Lee

Out of September it comes
as inescapable as the changing
of seasons we light
the Yahrzeit candle for you
father, at sunset, its soft
glow auspicious in the deepening
of evening and cry
believing tears a gift.
We whisper your name
as the flame leaps into life
and place the candle in a bowl
by the kitchen sink.
For years mother met us
in restaurants, on street corners
parking lots and hotel lobbies, until,
in the spring her own death grew
darker than yours.
In mother's unkept rooms we found
a shrine of photographs
and self-denial, bits and pieces
of you left in place amidst

the dust, you shone
behind glass, unwrinkled
wrapped in tissue paper; now
you are once again
in one another's keeping; for us
the years are punctuated by tears
and candle lightings.

A Common Womb: Sisters

– to Lee

So different now, like branches
spreading out
in opposite directions, groping
for the sky and yet
our blood flows from a single
tree, our roots
are anchored in the same
uncertain soil; what nourishment
there is feeds both of us
or neither; and if the weight of snow
should bend you, sister, till you feel the strain
too much to bear the pain
is mine as well, to wear; and if I break
in storm the wind will hurl
your anguished cry to where
I fall, we are as one, or we are
not at all.
Sister, in your heart there beats
a rhythm I have known, your eyes,
in fluid darkness saw, like mine,
the walls of our conception tomb

and not the graceless passages
of time, not death itself, can fell
the bonds of secrets shared within
a common womb.

Balancing

– for J.H.

Out there, somewhere, there is
a man
who has lost
the map to himself, he wanders
down other
people's streets, looking
in windows hoping
someone will recognize him.

The other day, I passed
myself in glass, looked up
and saw me walking
by my side; all the subtle
truths we whisper
when we wake desperately
alive at dawn, seemed
suddenly prophetic; time
is taut as wire and we walk
the wire for our lives.
Out there, somewhere, there is
a man who thought he'd found

salvation in someone
else's poem; grasped it
as he fell, to find he held
words empty
as air.

The Breath of Butterflies

– to Menke

Sunlight is real though
we know it not
by touch, by feel
the flesh is fed
the soul is nurtured into
love or sin or poetry; and stars
for all that they are bright
as flame are cold
and distant and beyond
the dreamer's reach and earth
and sky are ours to know
but never own the way
we own our destiny. Our lives
are streams that carry us
from place to place and gather
us at last into a vast uncertain
ocean of death; Menke,
you have found, along
your way, the crevices, flowed
into streams
seeped into cracks

of lives as dry as deserts
returned us to our dreams, gave us
back our tears; light
is a memory
that cannot fade, moisture dissipates
climbs its way to clouds to filter
down as rain, all things
that happen matter, large
or small, even butterflies
must breathe, their breath
your song; each rise
and fall a movement changing
in some way the rhythm
of the universe.

Calling the Angels

No, it is not at all
vanity my son. My end
is your beginning
I shall never be
stone-asleep, a sterile mute.
Silence is all song.
Hear next year's crickets
still in their eggs, serenade
all future autumns.
> *– Menke Katz (1906–1991)*
> *"Song"*
> *A CHAIR FOR ELIJAH*

I

At dusk I watched the slaughter
of the light, imagined how it died
beneath the fist
of night, breathless and bloody.
This morning, sunshine rolls around
the lawn like laughter, hugs the trunks
of trees, finger paints the leaves and I find

I disbelieve in darkness.
How can resurrection be
routine? How is it that we do not mourn
beyond our own small death of sleep; wake,
to clasp the promise of forever,
inherent in the morning, that we know
a few short hours will unkeep?

II

You taught us what there was to know of joy,
something whole that can be held
within an open hand. You taught that sighs
escape the heavens, are the distant voices
of the angels singing, and you
were intimate with angels, knew
the words to tempt them
to the table, called them
and they came, their merriment an echo
within the aftermath of glasses clinking
in an endless litany of toasts: "La Chaim!
La Chaim! To Life!" we chanted
and their voices adding
to our own filled up the room.

III

She was your lover; slept beside you naked
took you in to sleep and silence; kept,

for those few short hours, the words
at bay, so that you could rise refreshed
to embrace them.
They were your lovers too; each word quivered
like a virgin's breast beneath your mind's caress,
words seduced you with their innocence,
their lust, their raw need for you to bring
them to release and how you stroked
their passion into flame upon the page.
Inspiration was the substance of dust,
of weeds, of childhood dreams that burst
beneath the bombs of war; until your images
undid the gore and the shattered land
grew green again and dead men walked.
Aunt Beilke talked "the head
off death;" Rachel, the cow, gave cream;
"Yoodl the alley dancer" danced again
"for a crust of bread;" mothers tended
to their children's needs, all
the seeds of Michalishek bloomed
in the soil of your remembering.

IV

Indeed, light does not die; things come together
not in endings but beginnings, you knew that,
always, meant to tell us how darkness strokes
the thighs of light until they spread welcoming
the seed of morning.
Menke dead? Impossible! You visit me

in dreams and call the angels to my bed.
You said you had no time to die, your poems
holding you hard against life and so you bargained
with the angels, not for years, but days; a basket
full, a small unhurried row of hours, one day
of minutes and they gave you
every one; calling to you as you slept,
calling you, home.
And now we smile to know
not even angels dared
to keep you, Menke, from loving words
into one last poem.

Where Poets Go

– again to Menke

Late summer colored still
in tones of green slightly
fading is the flowers hymn, impatiens,
preened purple in the glare of August
hum in tones of late September
mauve, I think of you
      your voice held
up the hills, brought down
the sky in petals
of mist; this season hints
      at death, this season dies
like lust or leaves already
rushing to dry and test
the boundaries of themselves
in one first final
flight. You fly
      back from beyond where ever
tomorrow took you, if not heaven
then surely to a garden
where the flowers sing
bright chorus of all seasons

of all living things held
within the span
of your expanding wings.

For the Son of the Dead Poet

– to Dovid

Something of yourself
was spoken before
you were born breaching
the delicate balance
of your birth and his
grasp on eternity
       your minds
rhymed in the womb; he knew you
through her eyes, and as she grew
round within
you grew to the fullness
of words, lines
delicate as webs to hold you hard
against his heart, it was
       sanity, it was
that which filled his lungs
with song her gift
of you to him
that made the world
beautiful,
beautiful!

Blessings

– for my son, David

How could you have known
the night had always
touched you
softly and you woke
smiling to dawn.

> We could have told you
> how the water runs
> clear but deep
> beneath the surface
> there are things that crawl
> in silt and burrow in
> to mud to sleep.

Nothing ever stays
the same; not sorrow
and not joy, memories
do not define us, streams
of consciousness cannot
bind us to ourselves and lessons
learned, remembered, and believed

may, in the end, deceive.

> Now you fear the night
> too long, too cold, too
> empty of desire and move
> through dawn with little
> more than tendency
> to guide you.

Count the wounds
a blessing since, in time,
they too will heal, look
deep for truths
remembering the forest
generously treed, hides
more than it reveals.

The Call to Seasons

– for my daughter, Elizabeth

What wild things know is how
the seasons change and bring
them home; how bonds must never
bind, how blood
must not call to blood; we
break faith with instinct and forget
how to be free; 1000 miles away
you take to the skies and the air
around me begins to grow thin.

Trusting the Silence

I would seduce you with my silence if silence
were not in itself a lie; what does not speak
the truth, denies it and if there is no truth
then we must speak what masquerades as real; you
and I, different as night from day and yet
connected by the thrust of dusk or dawn, attached
like light to darkness by the threads of need; the seeds
of sight are nurtured blindly from the womb
I knew you in the way that water knows
the sand; the sensual caress of instinct,
your skin dancing against the center of my
self until you burst into the center
of our lives; my son,
we did not invent you, you
taught us who you are through all
the deeds and misadventures of your youth; the time
I slammed your finger in the car door and you barely
screamed and stayed the night cocooned
in pain your finger
swelling, throbbing, the nail, ink black and stretched
against the burst of blood, a simple pinprick loosened

in the morning. We learned you then
and time and time
again you caught our dreams of you off guard passing
them by; what now that you are grown; do we know less
of you, was something severed by the sharpness
of misunderstanding? Have we taken words
and turned them into stones, are we combatants in a war
for peace? We turn
the pages in our book nearing endings, your book
lays barely open in your hands, as you anticipate
beginnings. We are looking back through layers
of regret. What could we have told you,
what would you
have learned if we had known and knowing chose
to gift you with wisdom, possibility, conjecture; are we
come full circle back again to truths,
the argument for silence, is it still a lie;
could we convince you using love
as an excuse, is too much loving kindness
or abuse; can we believe you, will you believe us, do we
not still have some time together we can live; and
if we cannot speak aloud then surely, we must trust
the voice of silence to forgive.

My Map to God

– for Susie Katz Watson

We wondered in the softening
of April sunlight through the window
about the grace that children
place within our grasp.
You childless,
not by choice, tested cautiously,
my words with fingers
that had never known
the wrinkled flesh of birth
and there across the room
my sons seed grew
within the belly
of his wife, another life
happening beyond the scrutiny
of mind.
I found myself remembering
beginnings; the moment
when we first learn that we are not
alone, when something in us
moves to rhythms not our own,
so softly does it fill

the silence – that we swell
like song.
What words will take
you where I've been or duplicate
the ache that is both pain
and joy; there is
so much of sorrow
in delight and every gift
is priced according to its worth.
Your eyes insist and press
against me till your hurt
is mine; I want
to offer you whole
truth, to tell you what
I think I know, my son,
my daughter and their seeds
unborn are the name I call
myself, my map to God,
my soul.

The Wasted Space

– to Elizabeth

You came and filled the empty space
like sunlight fills a summer day
you tamed the ache and calmed
the fear when I would have bowed
to death you were the breath
that gave my lungs
a reason to rise.

How can I tell you how
it was when home
and duty called you
back and I woke to no commanding
voice instructing me to move to breathe
to eat to live the place you left
behind was like an empty frame
only your name stayed warm on my tongue.

So now you are there and here
is graceless an artless view
wasted the space
empty of you.

Devolution

– to my unborn grandchild

Sometimes in your grandfather's arms
I am drawn along
the liquid length of him
to source.
We fall
to the soil
that binds us
to ourselves
and memory.
We fall
by choice, to rise
implies to leave
behind, to rise
alone the sum
of something less
than whole,
falling
sliding with him
to a darkness not
beyond the possibility
of light where silence

is as startling
as sight we shed desire,
longing, need; devolve
our substance
to your seed.

Adventurer

– to David

You've loved the call
of mountains and the feel
of foam that tongued
a distant shore; watched far
from home a sunset's
flood of red and gold and felt
its flame define
your soul.
Now you are bound by chains
of innocence and need and home
is all the landscape
that you see; still, dreams
and promises begin like song
within the breast of birds, time
will unfold them and they'll gift you
with surprise: no black
New Zealand beach, no sunset
in Nepal can match the wonder
waiting as you turn the corner
of your daughter's eyes.

Why Cori Cries

– for Corinda

Her eyes, unfocused, trace
the patterns of the night, enfold
with dim awareness shadows breaking
into light, her breath moves
through her like the remnants
of a song, her skin is parchment pale, thin
as a sigh; and something
sound or substance, that we neither feel
or hear, makes Cori cry.
All joy that settles easily about her
as she sleeps, retreats into the cavern
of her wail, plaintiff, aching, anguished
who can name the essence of such
innocent despair and not
the grace of touching
not the voice that echoed
through pre-memory as Cori danced
within the waters of the womb, can
soothe her into silence.
Her body twists, her face contorts
into the tightness of a fist,

Cori's lament is loud
and adamant and lasts
until exhaustion teases
her limp.
We cannot claim to know for sure
for knowledge is a pond that fills
and empties at the whim of time,
born in a rush of blood and tears
and in a rush of tears to die,
yet must be taught to smile
or laugh and maybe that's
why Cori cries.

Dreaming: What We Dare

What We Dare

What we dare must be
worth it; all risks
are punitive.
The thorn hurts
out of envy, perhaps, because
it is not the rose which
soft and sensuous hardens,
on its way to death, to the texture
of thorn.
We harden around need
aching to be less
of what we are, more
of what we're not.
Do we dream ourselves whole
in memory or weave
new patterns to disguise
old mistakes and die
unrecognizable?
In the end,
what we dare must be
worth it, all risks
are punitive.

Resemblances

My dog kills rabbits; little
ones still nesting in warm
fur and brown grass; he stumbles
on them in the woods
behind our house and carries
them screaming like terrified
children onto the lawn; we try
to take them from him, but he turns
on us, his eyes growling possession,
his tongue heavy with fur
and blood, his thick liver-ticked
body trembling with the pleasure
of the kill.
For days afterward, I cannot
touch him, his eyes
follow me around the house, despairing.
He is only a dog, I tell myself,
knowing, it is not him I fear, but something
in him, that I see, primitive
and unthinkable that reminds me
of me.

The Pear Tree's Poem

"A poem should not mean
But be." – Archibald Macleish
"Ars Poetica"

The pear tree's blossoming
outside my window, each
slender limb encased in
whitening muffs of fragrance
that seem to drive the bees
to new heights of delight.
They move like dancers
down, around and through
the finery, a feast that fills
and leaves them wanting more.
Behind the sturdy stricture
of my window glass
I feel the censure
of a thinking world where
things are measured
by their meaning and their
worth.
In nature everything
keeps faith with simple

rules the tree
moves to the rhythm
of the wind, the bee moves
to the rhythm of the tree,
a harmony that does not mean
but is content
to be.

Wren and Song

The wrens returned again this spring
to nest within the wooden winter feeder
swinging from the maple's limb; impossibly
minute, the opening serves them now
for seasons beyond memory; smaller
than some snowflakes I have seen, they
stand their ground against all threats:
sparrow, blackbird, prowling tabby cat
and wake us every morning to the music
of their song; a sort of anguished challenge
hurled at dawn that reaffirms their lives
confirming that against all odds
they still survive.
I think of them as our wrens, the same
as last year coming home again, and yet
the likelihood is generations of them
lived and died; perhaps, no lineage at all connects
them year to year, just some coincidental
happening attracts a mating pair to our yard,
our feeder, convenient to their need,
and I suspect that we are not unlike them
in our journey through the centuries, we come
and go and pass this way or that and hurl, from

time to time the fact that we are here at all at
some deaf dawn; but in the grander plan
mattering not one bit less than wren and song,
not one bit more than here and gone.

The Mouse

The mouse has eluded
the trap beneath
the kitchen sink for three
nights in a row; the peanut
butter is gone, the trap
sprung and empty when I come
each morning to peek
behind the plastic can.
I picture his tongue
small and wet
as a snowflake teasing
the peanut butter
out from under the bar
the coil taut and tense,
his eyes wide
with the wonder
of what he does.
The dance must be
perfect, the timing delicate
as a sigh, the last lick
a flick of the tail
and the trap hurls
itself closed

on air.
Three nights
of such sorcery earns
him a life and the right
to leave his droppings
in the drawer.

A Greater Hunger

I

The snow's gone icy in the blow
of arctic air come down upon us
like a flight of angry birds; all night
beneath the covers, hovering beside
the warmth of some illusive dream I heard
the howling of the wind and windows
rattling like teeth against the cold.
This morning brightened silent
and still and everything turned
silver in the sun as though the stars
had settled in the drifts and now let
loose their light, the scene
was welcoming, compelling
as a call to prayer.

II

Outside the sun is overbright and bites
the skin, the crust of snow, fragile
as sand-scattered shells shatters
beneath my feet, icicles hang low like medals
on the bent and broken branches and behind
the snow-topped evergreen there is
a spill of blood and fur.
Some creature, smaller than my hand
died here last night. His eyes
swallowing a seed
his body huddling within
what warmth there was
in weighty pine had found a hunger
greater than his own and owl
or fox or pampered prowling cat enjoyed
the warmth against their tongue
of such a paltry feast.

III

For all the frigid air around me and
the silence that seems suddenly so loud
I burn with what can only be despair
here spread before
me on the ground is that bare truth
we clothe in fabrics of denial.
Death is impersonal and swift and leaves
of us this patch of anonymity spread

casually against a frozen span of years. I bend
and make a mound of snow to hide the little
that remains; to hide this small
indignity for what had been, at most
at least, a life
and cleanse the snow of stain.

Something Less than Perfect

The apple lay alone
in the woven wicker bowl; it's color
intensified by sunlight was the
green of watered summer lawns and in
my hand the feel
of it was silk and stone.
Along the rounded rim, a finger's width
from the core, the apple
bore a mark, small,
puckered, hard and black,
no more insinuating than
a sigh and still
my finger probed its
nonconformity, my eye detected, in its center,
so slight, it might have been
no hole at all, an opening that hinted
at the soft, white flesh within.
Something less than perfect
in the midst
of what seemed
whole, something
in us all along
the surface or beneath

the skin, a small
almost invisible door
that lets death in.

The Absence of Absolutes

If love is not light, then perhaps it is the absence
of absolute darkness, that which is, by mere degrees,
different than death.
Like the wolf's howl
that shatters silence into shards
of sound, so too, is love an opposite opposing
darkness with a glimmering
of flame, illuminating nothing
but itself, defining
in its flickering line
the subtle silhouette of shadow, the hue
of shade.
The heart that names itself
in love and quickens to the thought
of its salvation, instructs
the fingers toward delight releasing for
an instant the tightening knot
of night; throughout
the years that march
like armies past the heart's well-guarded
door, there is no absolute despair, memory,
a scrap of joy discarded there.

Retreat

Would that silence bloomed
like flowers in the mind, soft-
centered, delicate, the feel of satin
restless in the wind
of dreamless sleep,
no lies to shape
like clay into the lines of truth,
no promises to break
or keep and no excuses
to invent for all the flaws
and failings that the days heap
high as crusty leaves
about our feet.
Would that I could put the words
into the keeping of the poem
and then retreat
behind the blank
and wordless walls of home.

A Small Giving

The day rains thought; grey, fog-
shrouded and bleak and the world
seems desperate for something
that will speak a word reminiscent
of sunlight.
My words are brown
bark on winter wet trees; this is my
poem-song battered by the storm
of years, abraded by the promise
of mortality and each scab-
encrusted rhymeless line changes
nothing in the world though I ache
to have it matter.
Could I have understood
the substance of mathematics
or knelt to swab the sweat on patients'
faces greying onto death
I would have felt redeemed; but I
sit useless as fog, revealing
little, hiding little; we are only
what we are like seeds that grow
to blossom, or to weed, they follow
a line to the sun or shrivel in the quiet

dark to die unsung; we hope
to know the worth of what we do and settle
for the gifts that we are given, my hand
cannot heal, I cannot chart a course
to guide you through the stars, earth-
bound I harvest words to tell you
and myself that we are a part
of each other's pain; such a small
giving does not bring the sun, but may
deny the rain.

Façade

The Boston Fern did well all summer
on the patio, each coil stretching
out to point a finger coyly at the sky, who could
have guessed the winter death, brown, dry
as dust, that was the underside
of green, now stricken leaves fall
clenched like fists upon
the worn wood floor.

I revisit, white as vows, my wedding
gown packed in tissue, boxed
and sealed against the darkening
frigid mid-life days, fondling
the folds of memory my hands discover years
settled in the creases the insidious
decay to grey; beneath

your solid chest, where I have lain
in passion and in pain there is a heart
that beats to a measured
time and words that tie themselves
into a knot of promises
unravel into lies; we can

not claim possession, we borrow
everything; love, passion, arrogance; illusion
is the truth and most of what we see
facade; the centuries

will grind to dust the greatest
reach of stone, beneath
the blush of summer green
the roots of blooms collide
with bone.

Favors and Forgiveness

I used to bargain in the night
for favors and forgiveness and was surprised
by how the stillness never stirred; nothing
surprises me these days as I begin to roll
my eyes towards where I hope there is
a heaven; not passion or the absence
of it, not promises fulfilled
or broken, not the flighty path
of pleasure or the persistence
of pain.
The years are missed,
messy as a ballpark in
the aftermath of crowds, silence
seems louder for the memory
of cheers; yet there's a treasure
still upon the shelf, a bit
of time in which to learn
to forgive myself.

Changes

Nothing changes, nothing
stays the same each fall,
each resurrection records
itself, impermanent as light
reflecting off a glass eye.

> Hold me a moment
> in a thought pure,
> holy as an alter
> flame

> > I flicker
> > I die.

Memory holds its own, the tide
sings to the shore and the land
whispers a welcome; familiar
if not the same.

> So I recognize
> your touch in

> > the dark

> > in dreams.

Nothing changes, nothing
stays the same; beneath
the surface storm-tossed
and turbulent the waters

run calm, run deep only
the waves leap toward the promise

      of sky; angry
      or aching it is
            the same truth
            the same lie.

Non-Essentials

It is not necessary to know
where the wind comes from
or why silence is frightening:
what you cannot comprehend
speak of only in whispers, behind
your hands, into the fog.

It is not necessary to touch
death to know it is cold
and empty as eyes that open
into darkness; touch nothing
you cannot put
in your pocket.

It is not necessary to watch
dreams shatter like crusts
of ice beneath a heel, lock them
in boxes, keep them safe
from light, to dreams
we hold on tighter in the night.

It is not necessary to learn
that loneliness is essential, basic

as breathing, constant as stone; between
the solo journeys of birth and death let no one
in who promises to make you feel
less alone.

Stuck on the Couloir Lift

– Snowmass, CO.

I

At first, we were reminded
of the tomb, the fog was turbid,
a roiling mass that slithered
across the bare skin of our faces.
No sense of how high
we hung; no up, no down, minutes
meaningless as miles going nowhere,
suspended like bits
of beef in a thick broth.
We called, and waited, our voices
skipping like stones
over water, sinking
unanswered; the pole,
a cold chaperon,
queasy from the uneasy dip
and sway of the chair we felt
the vibrations of movement up
and down the line like a thin thread

binding us, all fear our own we leaned
gratefully into the knowledge,
we were not alone.

II

It is cold, a solemn, penetrating
cold that takes hold of fingers
and toes, they curl
into fetal knots, perception
numbs, we retreat into an inner
sense of self; I touch
the beating of my heart, feel
from the inside of each vein
and artery the steady, persistent
flow of blood as though
it is all of me that is
left alive.
At last, we are reminded
of the womb, the fog is amniotic,
we hear them, ten, twelve feet
below us calling, waiting in silence
waiting, for one of us
to answer.

No Scars

On board "Odyssey"
Gulf of Mexico

Moonlight mauls the Gulf Stream
waters held still
between the long
white hands of sand; through
the hull we hear the satisfied
grunts of fish eating barnacles
and seaweed off the bottom
of the boat; restless
in the pulse beat
of the tide, we dream
ourselves adrift like this
season of sun; sea song
is gull and splashing
tails of dolphins as they break
through layers of liquid light.
Life beyond scrambles
raggedly, a serrated blade
that saws at seams until
they bleed, the noisy life
that blasts disjointed sound

and ground that rumbles
threateningly beneath our feet.
We choose to live
that way and pay ourselves
in scraps like martyrs fasting
at a feast.
But here beneath a sky
engorged with stars, the elements
of time come
together like the healing
corners of a wound, cleanly,
leaving no scars.

Other Lives

A thousand times
a thousand lives
linger on this lip
of memory believing
themselves whole.

I have drifted to this shore
before, the scrabbled sand
is like a nest that holds
the scent of birth, the sky
pinned to itself by stars
that relieve themselves
of light, the wind blowing
my name.
I cannot count the times
I've stumbled
on myself, come back
through tunnels, through
trails overgrown with shadow
through water that moved
without intention
from shore to shore.
We move, holding ourselves

together with what we label
dreams, toward horizons,
toward crests that loom beyond
the flight of birds muttering
small relevancies as though
we owe a debt we cannot pay.
And in the end, the fusion
of land and sky, is always just
beyond our reach, the mountains
clamor toward a sky that swallows
them in mist, oceans heeding
the pull of gravity, carry us
like seeds back
to beginnings…

> toward silent lives
> that are our own,
> toward other lives
> that leave us
> less than whole.

At the Supermarket
Checkout Counter

"… FBI insiders swear Kennedy
is alive!" Weekly World News 2/24/92
…the tabloid headlines read:
JOHN F. KENNEDY STILL LIVES

...and claimed he lingers, crippled
and bound
to a wheelchair in an undisclosed
retreat; a picture, hazy and unclear
evidenced the fact.
I pondered, only briefly, gullibility and how
our need for headlines allows that anything
and everything is real and then
forgot
the incident until today
when reading headlines of a world
that hungers after war, starves
for food and thrives
on hate and avarice and all the multiplicity
of things that make the fabric
of our world too coarse
to wear, too thin

for warmth; raggedly,
we've come these years
since the shot
rang out
and history happened on a Dallas street.
Perhaps
the kernel of absurdity
is truth
the seed of truth
the greater lie
the bullet struck
and just
perhaps
Kennedy lives
and the whole world died.

Common Dead

Touring the English countryside
– June/1990

The sky is oozing grey again today, the tarnished
grey of ancient armor stiffly at attention
in the corners of old manor homes and castle keeps,
beneath an endless canopy of clouds, the countryside
is lush and greenly thrives, each bush and blade
of grass satisfies a gluttonous thirst and flowers
burst like bubbles through the seams
of rocks.

The stones of abbeys rise, bones up from
the elegance of meadows, break to dust
along the banks of hurrying streams; faces
fade back into rock that once surveyed these
same bucolic scenes with arrogance or eyed
the heavens with a thought toward prayer or
faced eternity, locked by a nameless sculptor's
hands, into a pose of dreams.

Upon the hills that look to be an endless row of heads
bowed humbly in penitence, sheep graze white-faced,

blue-faced, black-faced they dream-walk through
the centuries, mindless of their own
demise as though each walk a path
set down before we numbered hours
between sun's set, sunrise.

History is strewn as carelessly as wind-borne
seeds, full-blown or long since buried by a shifting
landscape to reappear beneath a farmer's
plow: Here's Hastings where unlucky Harald
fell and William grasped the handle
of the world and turned it to his will, roses,
draped like veils along a wooden fence, drip
scarlet petals nurturing the battlefield turned
meadow; and there: Hadrian's wall rises
and falls like a river carved in stone, palaces
and castles hurl their permanence like gauntlets
in the face of time; Beaumaris, flat and fierce embraced
by cold sea winds, Cannarfan, Sudeley, and Leeds lovely
as a lady dressed in silk out for a Sunday stroll,
and everywhere, within the fading walls
of churches, out along the mossy paths, bent
broken falling to the black soil, transparent
as tears; tombstones, history's heartbeat, name
names, give centuries their soul: HERE LIES…
all that remains of mothers, daughters, fathers
sons; dates, like candle flame hold
back the dark abyss of night; alongside Harald
in that field, that day, men died, whose names
still hovered on the lips of lovers
and mothers cried.

Each epitaph, anonymously yields a name
that history ignores, and tells more
of who we are and what our destiny must be
then all the battles fought, and all the heroes gone
to dust; the common dead sleep silent sleep, only
their restless dreams whisper through the lush
grass beneath the bowed heads of grazing sheep.

In the End

    Deny
nothing, not even
the ache that borders
on bruising.

    Display
the scars, small
maps that remember
where your life
has been.

    Despair
the smooth skin
that lacked
a destination.

Dreaming: The Reasons Why We Bleed

The Reasons Why We Bleed

– for the 3000 in Tiananmen Square

Let us speak of blood
and the reasons why
we bleed; the vain
and indiscriminate thrust
the greed, the lust; a man
should recognize the eyes that speak
his death, should have a name
to hurl at his eternity, but men
die strangers or worse, alone,
their death comes
at them, out of nowhere,
like a curse.
Let us speak
of blood, we spill a river
and the red tide rises
to a flood, for want
of reasons we wage wars
and call them causes, compile
a list of dissidents, dissenters, label
them disease and cut
them like a cancer from

our common flesh and never
feel the pain.
Blood speaks its pain
in puddles on our city streets
in parks, in squares, and out
along the quiet country roads
where voices dare
believe aloud their dreams.
Speak of blood
and of the silent
dead, speak
aloud and louder
still until their silence stills
the slaughter
with its screams.

Reversal

Because, he said he was
"under loved" he shot
his mother
five times
in the back,
spewed bullets that birthed
blood in puddles
on the wooden
floor; five times
his fingers labored
at the trigger easing
back, the gentle pulsing
of a single finger sterilized
the years as though
through this
penetration of her, he could crawl
between the torn
flesh and become
unborn.

The Unbending

"Ashland, Ohio – An Ohio mother of a three-year old who came to be known
as Ashland County's Lost Boy' after his body was discov-
ered along a highway
...told police his last weeks were filled with beatings, and abuse. she accused
a male companion of repeatedly hitting the child in an effort to make him cry."

He couldn't make you cry
though trying was a ritual
of fists, through days
that closed behind you
loudly like the slamming of a door.
She was there,
a shadow among shadows
staring like a statue past
your pain and praying maybe,
you would break and cry and
he would satisfy himself
with that.
But you were like a sponge,
absorbing broken bones

and bruises, nothing spilling
out of those dry eyes, and he
would stare into their silence
and become undone.
It was almost like a bargain
struck between you, man and boy,
he swearing he would bend you
to his will, she would see you cry,
you thriving on the need
to soundlessly endure,
and with your lips,
still holding back the roar,
you died.

Forty North Main Street

In the uneven light
streets look bruised, houses crouch
wary as stray dogs, windows tragic
in their vacant stare; streets
are rutted,
grown tricky in their weaving
through back lots, past shuttered
stores, a week
sooner, before the clock shifted,
you might have sidled in light
past the spot waiting
to absorb your death, or hurried
instead of stopping for a soda
at the grocery store, a minute more
or less; the blow
unhinges everything, dragging you
down into a coarse silence; your held breath
bursts, hands take you
into the bushes, take you
out of yourself into
a new knowledge and you move
sideways out of the old life; the knife
finds you virginal, claws

past fantasies of how
it would be, demands more
than virtue can protect; you sink
into a sanity of your
own where there is
no fear, where the streets are morning
streets, houses curled
softy around their own corners,
doors open like smiles, blossoms
obliterate whole patches of sky, sprinklers
blind the eye and shortcuts lead
to candy stores; around you
the town moves inside itself, yawning,
stretching, settling towards sleep,
televisions hum, girls whisper
into telephones and pastel pillows,
their laughter losing itself
among the leaves; a dog barks,
smoke drifts across the sky, unseen
your arms and legs detach themselves
and twitch like puppets,
struggling, you break
the thin line that binds you
in time and move, digging in
to what you will take with you
of pain, they find you
partially covered
by leaves, your face quietly set,
your eyes unlit, your body strangely
out of grace, as though weary
you had merely paused

in search of sleep; only your lips
deny the pose, locked against secrets
tomorrow's headlines will unkeep.

The Dart Man

He is coming for you
            Lady
while you are rolling the taste
of evening across your tongue
easing your way past shadows
towards sleep.
            He is coming for you
swelling with need all eyes
stalking the night that is settling
over your dreaming.
            He is coming for you
this watcher
at open windows fondling
you with his eyes rubbing
across your flesh stroking
you into a frenzy
in his mind.
            He is coming for you
feeling himself
triggered
stinging you with the steel
of his longing withdrawing

sated and soiled
into the night.

Stargazer

Embassy Row Hotel
Washington, D.C.

Below my window the world crawls
cautiously as crabs as the tide
deserts them.
What washes away leaves
bare an uncertain tolerance
for circumstance.
Trucks torment blacktop, taxis
hoot insults indiscriminately
and at a glass enclosed metrobus
stop a lone figure, subdued
in the caress of early evening eyes
with binoculars my hotel window.
Looking for what behind
the carelessly drawn drapes
of paisley? Lives happening
here as unreal as moon men kicking
up dust at Tranquility Base; I am
defined by that impersonal stare.
We are always, only, part
of one thing at a time; today,

he is stargazer hoping
for discovery, I am
compelled to show him
something, a bare
breast, buttocks, something.
The moment is brief, tides
turn back, planets move toward
unreachable destiny, I let
the light hold
me; it is a small
gift, he will make of it
what he will, slipping
into shadow tonight, if he chooses,
he may name
a new universe.

The Doctor's Death

– for B.V.

Your hand slid over the swelling
of my lower back, knowing
its deception, *"like an old mattress"*
you said, *"you grow lumpy: a question
of things rearranging themselves, grow
accustomed to new contours;"* you
patted my hand and we both smiled.
How is it that you, who knew the enemy,
unmasked it often enough in the limp-lidded
stare or the loose cough, didn't sense it
shading your steps?
Your hands had often paced
my pulse, probed my belly where
a gall bladder grew grouchy,
sat with me while I gasped
at the raw ache of the surgeon's aftermath,
vacillating on Valium between two temples
of pain. You prescribed low-fat meals
and petroleum jelly.
Now it all comes back, rising
out of your grave, the lump

swells and begins to feel
real, the ache is acidic
again. I want more
of you, need to know why you fought
my battles and surrendered your own,
wonder, if in a terror to transfer
my death into your hands, I might not
somehow, have killed you.

The Waiting

The impossible quiet
in this funereal room
mirrors the smile
fixed, on his waxen face.
Black-draped frames
stain the walls,
as if to prove
he'd really lived.
Like some gigantic bird
roosting on a gray
metallic folding chair
she mourns her son.
There is a momentary stir,
hands scoop her off the floor,
unfold her bulk
and lean her back
against the polished wood.
Her fingers stiff
inside her mourning gown
roam the satin of his sheets.
Her unrouged lips, ghost slits
against her swarthy skin,
pursue some old-world prayer.

Behind closed eyes,
he bides his time,
waiting for the hovering to cease
the lid to close,
the necessary privacy to decompose.

The Hold of Stone:
The Corpses at Pompeii

Death engulfed them, took them with
their eyes open staring at the black
side of Hell, took them screaming, took
them, like children by the hand, through
the whole long
moment of dying.
The night was fire, smoke
and ash and air so hot
lungs blistered and everything
common, everything known became
the strange shape of shadow and there was
no light and there was no
escape, no place
to hide, no place
to fall through.
And in fear
and in terror and in
need they ran
they climbed, they
crawled until the world
stopped, heavy
and empty of air and they were bound

in rags of ash in coffins
of stone fitting them like skin holding
in their bones, in poses held
like a breath, seeming to need only
an instant more
for them to unfold.
And the centuries were
cold and cautious and the dead
lay deep beneath volcanic silence
beneath the sweet
blue sky and the white
warm winds that swept
in from the sea, until reclaimed they
now speak from the safety of glass
cases with their eyes
with their hands, with the twisting
torment of their bodies and their
mouths open.
What they do not speak is locked
inside the minds that died whole,
were caught with thoughts intact.
What could we know
what could we learn
what could be told
if we could hear
beneath the hold of stone.

Blessing

It takes no more or less than this to lose
everything the soft expulsion of a breath
all the certainty of life
reversed to death; it takes
the very least we have to give
a sigh, the fluttered opening
of an eye to live, not monuments
and not eternity may name
us blessed, but
that we were and are
no more, no less.

Dreaming: The Lie of Leaving

The Lie of Leaving

I

Together we have come
in winter when the ground
is hushed beneath the white
breath of angels and trusted
in the hope of spring,
     come
in spring like rain
to the soil and watched
it ripen on yesterday's bones,
     come
like babies suckling
at the full breast of summer
till it succumbs to fall
     came
at us with regret, taking
without giving, promising
nothing…

II

Breathless you came in fall
quoting lines that mapped
the road to your heart, insinuating
possibilities and all the world
hardened suddenly to frost, constricting
logic, lessons, acquiescence
meek surrender.

III

Death is not faceless, is not
a quiet space between
the seasons where we slip
like dust to blow away,
death demands
departure, ritual, the spoken prayer
an earthy glow or glowering before
we dry and crumble to despair,
a moment focusing and we,
like trees that turn in fall to colors
far beyond their ordinary garb, need
to preen for the mirror of the sky, cast
a desperate plea to a heaven far
too far away to hear,
to name us, hold us holy till we shed
our leaves like tears.

IV

And what if what
the words we said were true; could we
have said goodbye politely, let the lie
of leaving bring us quietly to stand
back-to-back and walk away
like strangers, an unvoiced scream
echoing throughout the shattered years?
You cannot simply take
your leave of me, for in the time
between the lie and its unfolding, I found
I do not know the way
to let you go.

Afterward

When our breath had slowed and our fingers
cooled flesh that moments earlier
had flamed, I said, "I love you;" then
disclaimed the words as not
enough: you said, "We have no need
for words."
Ah, love… you are a man
of action taking with your grasp and bending
with the groan of muscle and the grunt
of bone, the task at hand; I am a woman, words
the messengers of my soul.
Your soul has words
for what your fingers speak, reach
deep until they surface, writhing
on your tongue, say them
slowly, watch
my eyes.
Sometimes words enlarge the pupils
of your eyes till they surround
my face like an embrace and I am sure
your voice aches to color them
with sound.
When I am all alone and memory

hangs loose upon me
like a shawl; words, solid as walls
keep the night at bay; you do not need
the words I speak; when I am all alone, I seek
the words you do not speak
to keep me warm.

Greening Alone

The leaves
August-engorged hang
heavy under the weight
of such stout air, we wade
like swimmers through
the seas
of summer, hazy
hot and humid – the air
suspends everything
in a separate space and sound
slows as it finds us
bent beneath the ache
of love; old,
as summer folds slowly
into fall; love
touch me now my skin
is wet with wanting
you; what will we do
in winter,
in winter when the wind
dries us to bone
and spring comes to find us
greening alone.

The Fog

– on board "Winderful" 7-21-89

The fog is intimate
and like a lover
lures us
laves us
with a wild
wet tongue
then leaves us
lost and lusting
for the warm
impersonal caress
of sun.

In the Name of Love

Tonight, it is your triumph
that quiets to
the grey gauze
of sleep, claiming
the light that burned
in your eyes.
And the words that hung
between us
like a gallows rope,
tightening, lose themselves
like rain in swollen
rivers.
I hold between defeat
and sleep the only truth
I dare believe and take it
with me past the crust
of dreams, nightly we kill
each other in the name
of love and in
the name of love wake
to grieve.

Borrowing

What we have done
is take a little
from each other,
just enough to firm
the days, to spread
a little light
into the darkest corner
of the longest night.
What we have done
is pick at bits and pieces
of each other's flesh,
to cover up our wounds,
to hide the scars time
has pasted on our faces.
What we have done
is take a little
with our eyes,
our fingers and our mouths
until we taste, way back
on our tongues, the salt
of one another's weeping.

The Parting

Your fragrance lingers
in the closet, on the pillow
by my head; yesterday's
roses unfold
in the dark, their fragrance
stale but persistent; perhaps
tomorrow I will wake
to find their petals scattered,
edging to brown.
I believe that when the stem
is cut the flower
dies you should have stayed
a little longer, I think
I needed to see the light
go out in your eyes.

Halfway to Nowhere

Distance separates us from ourselves
and one another; divide a space in half
and half remains, we come
together but we never
touch, imagination fuels
our passions and incites
our fantasies to bridge
the gap.
We meet halfway
to nowhere, like a dream begun,
unfinished by our waking; the game
is played out in our heads, our hands
hold air, our fingers feel
what isn't there.
What's real is what we think
is real and if space halves
itself then so must time and death's
preposterous since nothing stops
and nothing starts and if
we cannot meet
we cannot part.

The Unwounding

Passion is an arrow that leaves
the quiver in a hush
of sound and tests itself
against the bow, released, it rapes
the air of innocence in bloodless flight
takes the flesh with steel and ends
it's thrust in bone.

The heart is innocent of subterfuge, subtle
secrets and deceit; it's not unlike a flower welcoming
the rain or warming to the sun; it does not question
gifts that come unasked for and cannot separate a lie
from that which calls itself the truth,
but youth that argues for the prize of passion
had best observe the flower as it fades, summer's
gaudy colors turn to bitter brown and break
against the wind, scattering to decay; the heart
that would survive the seasons, like the flower
needs the sustenance of soil, the comfort
of that passionless embrace in which to store
its seeds beyond the reach
of winter's kill.

The heart is neither stone nor flower
it beats a time and then for all eternity is still
and in the breathless flight of that brief hour would
do well to know, one cannot unwound the flesh
unless the arrow never
leaves the bow.

Dreaming: You

You

You
were the hands that kept me
from myself in the long nights,
framed my days with sturdy
promises,
tramped ahead leaving me
your shadow to hold onto.

You
shouted louder, your anger
diminishing mine; in the heat
of your touch, I found forgiveness.

You
restless, now, in the thin
hours before dawn
when the mind
holds like a mirror the
reflection of itself
were afraid of secrets
and success; have the years
made of me more or of you
less?

Regret

It is twenty-seven years
      since we
moved into one
      life – since
I came
      to your bed
and your eyes
      defined me.
A hundred miles apart
      I would be able
to taste
      you on my tongue,
accommodate the pressure
      of your thighs.
A thousand years
      from now
there would be spaces
      still in the course
of your touch –
      unfinished rhyme
I would be learning
      I regret nothing

\- but the lack
of time.

Morning's Blood Song

Light –
       fingers that part
the hair-strands of the
willow, patterning the ground
like scripture
on stone.
Light –
       mellow as morning's
blood song blushing
over the cheeks of summer
meadows; flowers
blossoming like laughter
out of the mouths of children.
Light –
       darting like fish between
flecks of foam, caught
on the crests of waves, rhyming
the tides into
a wordless poem.
Light –
       a million times
a million stars, burning
God-Eyes, our prayers

preening in their silver stare.

Light –
        candle-flame
on your lips
in your hair, drawn
by more than memory, your touch
in the midst of midnight's
menace, the salve
of dawn.

No Trace

In the mirror, in
the morning, I see
like the clear reflection of trees
in calm waters, traces
of faces I see
now
only in dreams; the slant
of an eye, the pinch
of a lip
into a crooked smile
In the night, you, who hold
what I am, bending beneath
its weight like pines
beneath the cautious crush
of snow, test
the waters of sleep and the heart
that hurts with passion hurries
back to its own rhythm and the night
swallows the silence.
In passion we took
and left
something of ourselves, skin,
sweat, scent, nourishing

as rain those drops that keep
the rivers of ourselves
from running dry and hold
us whole till
morning.
In the morning, in the
mirror, I see the proof
of passion in my dead
mother's eyes, my dead
father's smile, no trace
of you whose touch
pried loose the jaws of night and
kept me alive.

This Is a Happy Poem

Because...
sadness blends everything
grey, the soft grey of winter
clouds and pussy willows, the blur
of hummingbird's wings,
          since dawn a small
red-headed woodpecker has orchestrated
morning and the vinca vine growing
in the oak planter has resisted
winter's kill, the house is still
and faintly wood-smoke fragrant.
I woke remembering sleeping
in the concave shelter of your embrace
and found etched in feathers
the merest outline
of your face.
Old photographs, beside the bed, have faded
past the point of pain, dead names, in prayers,
roll lightly off my tongue,
because...
last night your eyes
were still young.

Night Finder

There are those who make
discoveries at night, who
shift the darkness through
a filter and find light.
In an aching ebony of dreams
so fragile and so far, night
finder you remind me that the dark
has little substance and beyond…?
The stars!

How It Is with You

You are summer's
silence; bright sunlight
off the leaves – drunk with dew,
a study
in coarse contrasts, puckered
and peeling like weathered
bark on old
old trees, something non-transient
to believe in; it is
never the truth
of things that touch
us; rain is real,
but heavy-handed; mist,
ethereally suspends us
in the substance of itself it is
like that with you,
your name a seed
blossoming
on my tongue.

The Simplicity of Silence

You are the simplicity of silence,
a study in thoughts
that begin deep, swelling
like the huge rollers that cross
the Atlantic and speak
only a murmur
to the shore; more than that,
line, texture, form
so clean it takes my breath away
when I confront your face
in sleep and trace
the landscape of your body hard
beneath the sheet.
Words test nothing more
than patience, lies color
the scene like fall leaves, dying
even as they're spoken and promises
are remembered, if at all,
when they are broken; but you
are more an aftermath
of storm or changing season, you
happen to me, offering
in your silence

all the certainty of rhyme
and sanity
of reason.

The Play

What your fingers tell me
of myself is startling
as sun on snow, unsettling
as if you read
my skin like braille.
You seek me
with your hands, your mouth
your tongue and every stroke
names me, answers
all the riddles of my place
in time and space; within
your arms I am
as malleable as clay
with your knowledgeable
touch teach me
the line, together
we'll enact the play.

When You're Not Here

All ways your memory shapes
itself into the dim brown
circling of dreams and in
between the settling dusk and innocent
allure of dawn I try to warm myself
against your touch
remembered and the flesh
that quivered with delight absorbs
you like darkness
swallows light.
Once you told me, "Silence
is a sound unspoken, pregnant
as the promise of spring rain;" but I
cannot enfold the world in some
unspoken certainty
see green and growing where still
the earth is torn and broken
and when I close
my hand around the need, the seed will
not suffice; I must abrade myself
against the permanence of bark.
How can I make you know
the price of such necessity; rain,

not promises persuade
the flowers to grow, without
the real invasion of your hands, your body
pressing flesh to bone all heat, love
passion dissipates and I grow cold
as stone.

Collision

– for Don always

Einstein said that death dissolves us,
spreads us like a mist
back into the sea. I understand
the theory in my head,
that we are all a part of something bigger
than ourselves; that nothing starts or stops
just for an instant moves a bit apart
from all the rest; but in that instant
you and I collide, and know the need
of boundaries on the skin that fingers
might define; explain
to what I call my heart,
thrown back into the soup of time,
how I will bear
the parting pain.